D1065332

In Search of

KNOSSOS

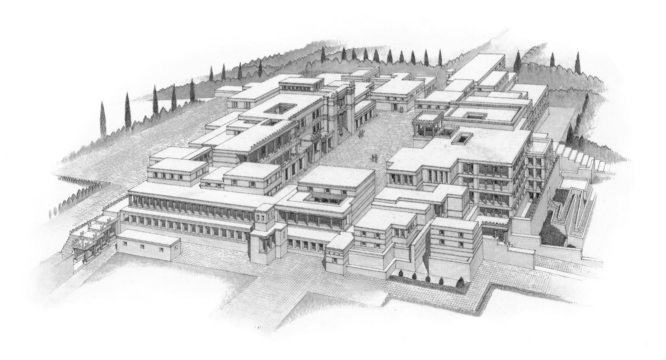

In Search of
KNOSSOS

The quest for the Minotaur's labyrinth

Written and illustrated by
Giovanni Caselli

PETER BEDRICK BOOKS
New York

For Emily

Published in the United States in 1999
by Peter Bedrick Books
A division of NTC/Contemporary
Publishing Group, Inc.
4255 West Touhy Avenue
Lincolnwood (Chicago), Illinois 60646-1975
U.S.A.

Library of Congress Cataloging-in-Publication Data

Caselli, Giovanni, 1939-
  In search of Knossos : the quest for the Minotaur's labyrinth / written and illustrated by Giovanni Caselli.
    p. cm. -- (In search of)
  Includes index.
  Summary: Describes the discovery and excavation of Knossos by the archaeologist Sir Arthur Evans and what the site revealed about the Minoan civilization that flourished on the island of Crete from about 3000 to 1150 B.C.
  ISBN 0-87226-544-7 (hardcover)
  1. Crete (Greece)--Antiquities Juvenile literature. 2. Knossos (Extinct city) Juvenile literature. 3. Palace of Knossos (Knossos)-- Pictorial works Juvenile literature. 4. Evans, Arthur, Sir, 1851-1941--Contributions in archaeology Juvenile literature.
  5. Excavations (Archaeology)--Greece--Crete Juvenile literature.
  [1. Crete (Greece)--Antiquities. 2. Knossos (Extinct city)
  3. Evans, Arthur, Sir, 1851-1941. 4. Excavations (Archaeology)-
  -Greece--Crete.] I.Title. II. Series.
PQ151.C37   1999
939'.18--dc21   99-28013
                                                        CIP

Printed in Hong Kong / China

International Standard Book Number:
0-87226-544-7

99 00 01 02 03 15 14 13 12 11 10 9 8 7 6 5 4 3 2 1

Acknowledgments

The author and publishers would like to thank Judith Lange, Rome, for use of the photographs on pages 36-37.

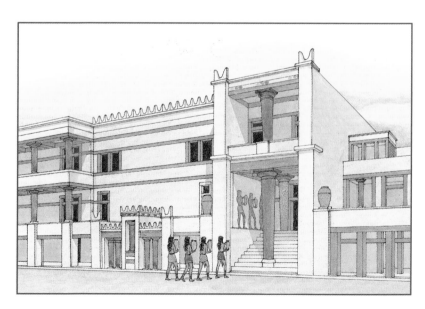

Contents

The Minotaur of Crete

According to Greek legend, Minos was the ruler of the island of Crete at the dawn of time. He received a gift of a beautiful bull for sacrifice to Poseidon, the great god of the sea, but his wife liked the bull so much that Minos decided to keep it. Poseidon was furious and as an act of revenge made Minos's wife give birth to a monstrous child, half-human, half-bull. The monster was called "Minotaur," which means "Minos's bull."

The king kept the Minotaur in a huge indoor maze called a labyrinth, which he had built close to his palace. Every nine years the Minotaur received a sacrifice of seven boys and seven maidens from Athens, a city on mainland Greece, which Minos ruled. The Minotaur hunted the young people through the passages of the labyrinth before killing them.

When a young Athenian prince called Theseus could no longer endure his country's awful tribute, he volunteered to sail to Crete and kill the Minotaur.

King Minos?

Was King Minos a real man? Most scholars believe that "Minos" was a royal title, like "Pharaoh" in Egypt. These heads (above) were thought to represent Minos and his son.

A maze of passages

The rambling layout of the Palace of Knossos was designed to confuse the unwary visitor. In ancient Crete, this palace maze was known as the "House of the Double Ax," which meant labyrinth. The ancient labyrinth (above) is scratched on a clay tablet.

Greek vase

This vase of the 6th century BC is painted with a scene from the Minotaur legend. Theseus is shown killing the Minotaur, watched by some of the youths who would have been the monster's victims.

As Theseus set foot on the island, his eyes met those of Ariadne, King Minos's beautiful daughter. It was love at first sight.

Ariadne gave Theseus a sword and a ball of yarn. She told him to tie a thread to the entrance of the labyrinth and uncoil it as he made his way along the winding passages. After slaying the Minotaur, Theseus followed the thread back through the maze to safety. That night, he sailed back to Athens with Ariadne by his side.

Two sides of the story

The coins of Crete often commemorated the legend of Theseus and the Minotaur. One side of this 5th-century BC coin shows the running monster, half-human and half-bull; the other depicts the labyrinth.

Battle to the death

With strength and cunning, Theseus managed to overpower and kill the hideous monster in the heart of its lair (below).

Finding Knossos

When archaeologist Arthur Evans (1851-1941) traveled in search of valuable antiquities, he became fascinated by the small gemlike seals he saw throughout the Greek islands—especially on the island of Crete.

In 1894 Evans was in Crete looking for more seals when he came across the vast ruin of the Palace of Knossos. He made up his mind to excavate the site. He was interested in the truth behind the legend of King Minos and the Minotaur, as well as in discovering the civilization that had developed the writing on the seals.

Evans purchased the land from the government of Crete in 1899 and began excavations on the site in 1900.

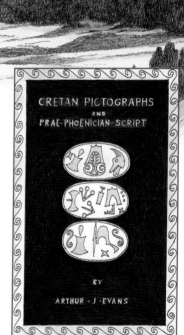

Evans at Oxford
Arthur Evans began his career as a journalist but through his interest in classical antiquities quickly became a curator at the Ashmolean Museum in Oxford.

The stones of the islands

Some of the seals Evans found showed hunting scenes and some showed dolphins or ships; others carried what appeared to be inscriptions in an unknown writing.

Tiny gems
Evans's nearsightedness may have made him more appreciative of the tiny seals that he had to bring close to his eyes to examine.

Evans, the collector

Cretan hieroglyphics
Tablets found by Evans on Crete bore marks that may have been written characters. In 1900 Evans published a book (right) on Cretan pictographs and writing.

CRETAN PICTOGRAPHS
AND
PRAE-PHOENICIAN-SCRIPT

BY
ARTHUR · J · EVANS

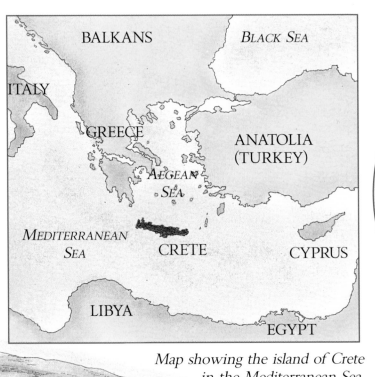

Map showing the island of Crete in the Mediterranean Sea.

Before arriving in Crete, Arthur Evans excavated ruins in the Balkans.

From the ashes

Work to uncover Knossos started on March 23, 1900 at 11 A.M. Evans's team consisted of 32 workmen and a foreman. They were soon to reveal a vast ruin—a palace several stories high, with a maze of rooms, courtyards and storerooms on the enormous site. As the digs progressed, it became apparent that the palace had been at the center of an important ancient civilization, the Minoans.

Evans talks to a Cretan authority at the site.

13

Uncovering the past

The excavation work at Knossos lasted for 35 years. Evans was advised by D. G. Hogarth and Duncan Mackenzie, both experienced archaeologists. During the first five seasons (until 1904), Evans was also helped by Theodore Fyfe, the architect of the British School at Athens, who was replaced in 1905 by Christian Doll, who helped Evans reconstruct parts of Knossos.

The Grand Staircase was rebuilt with the help of miners and the foreman, Gregorios Antoniou, a Cypriot who had assisted Evans at the site since 1902. He also obtained the services of a Swiss artist called Emile Gillieron and his son Edward. Together they restored the beautiful wall paintings at the palace.

Evans insisted that the workforce should include both Muslims and Christians, and Mackenzie made sure that this was so.

The journals kept by Evans record that in 1900 the average wage for a day's work at the site was eight piasters or one shilling and four pence (about fifteen cents today, although this sum bought a lot more in 1900 than it does now).

On location
The above picture shows Evans (at lef Mackenzie, Fyfe and a group of Creta laborers standing on the Grand Stairca

Men at work
Evans's team started to dig in the southeast corner of the palace's West Wing and worked north. At one time as many as 300 people were at work on the site. Here, workers excavate the palace's Throne Room. The throne itself is visible behind the workers, situated against what would have been a wall.

Bird's-eye view
As the excavations progressed on the hillsid at Knossos, the palace buildings started to emerge from the ruins and the Throne Room's roof was reconstructed.

Hundreds of clay tablets were found in the ruins of Knossos. They were inscribed with the same mysterious symbols that Evans had seen on the seals he had discovered earlier. He had found what he had set out to find—a civilization with its own form of writing, unique customs, art and architecture and a sophisticated economic system. He also uncovered evidence of magnificent pottery and metalwork.

Giant pot

When the storerooms were excavated, they were found to contain enormous food storage vessels, some taller than a person. The pots had many handles to make them easier to move.

Telltale symbols

The discovery of Egyptian seals gave clues to the date of Knossos.

Egyptian seal

Fabulous finds

Evans made a note of all the discoveries at Knossos. He also sketched designs, patterns, and plaques showing house styles that he found at the site.

Evans holding a vessel found at Knossos.

15

Palace on the hill

  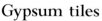

The vast building that Arthur Evans called "The Palace of King Minos" lies on a gentle slope that runs down to the ravine of a narrow stream. This leads to the harbor and the sea.

From a distance the palace would have been an impressive sight. People coming from inland approached by the South Entrance, those coming from the harbor by the North Entrance. Private rooms were situated in the East Wing, which Evans called "The Domestic Quarter." Across the Central Court, the West Wing consisted of shrines and cult rooms, and probably the state apartments. Baths, waterfalls and pools adorned the palace.

Gypsum tiles

Tiles made of gypsum (a mineral used to make plaster) paved and decorated the floors and walls of the palace's stately rooms. Seats, thrones and staircases were also made of, or finished with, gypsum.

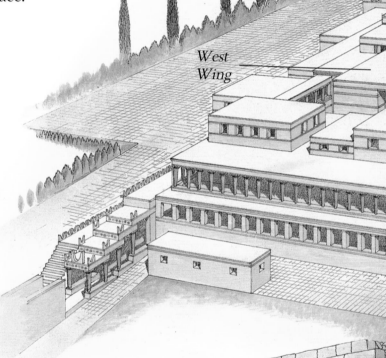

West Wing

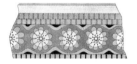

Wall frieze from the palace

Walls of the palace were made of masonry and braced with timbers

A colorful colonnade

Columns were made from the polished trunks of pine trees. The trunks were turned upside down and the lower and narrower part rested on a stone base. The wooden capital (top of the column) supported a roof beam.

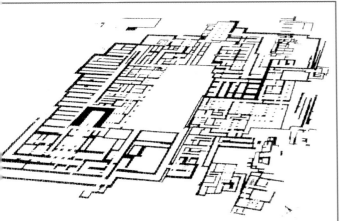

On a grand scale

This is how the palace would have looked in 1500BC. Cellars, staircases and colonnades (rows of columns) were all creations of Minoan architects, who were probably influenced by Syrian rather than Egyptian buildings.

Gypsum floor tiles

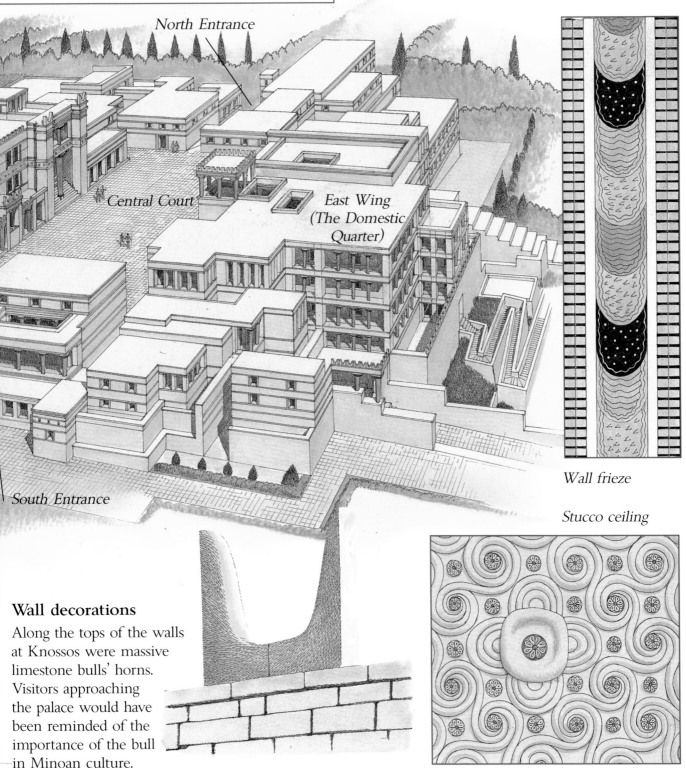

North Entrance

Central Court

East Wing (The Domestic Quarter)

South Entrance

Wall frieze

Stucco ceiling

Wall decorations

Along the tops of the walls at Knossos were massive limestone bulls' horns. Visitors approaching the palace would have been reminded of the importance of the bull in Minoan culture.

The royal quarters

In its heyday, about 1600BC, the Palace of Knossos was a magnificent structure. The East Wing, with its great halls, luxurious apartments, bathrooms and shrines, was the royal residence.

Underneath, a warren of passages and corridors led to vast storerooms and workshops stuffed with treasures. There were also elaborate tombs and a dazzling array of murals (wall paintings).

The royal apartments in the East Wing included state rooms such as the King's and Queen's "megarons," or reception halls, the Queen's bathroom, and the Shrine of the Double Axes. The Grand Staircase leading to the upper floors was decorated with colonnaded terraces.

Fit for a queen

In the Queen's megaron, bright murals of dolphins and other sea creatures decorated the walls.

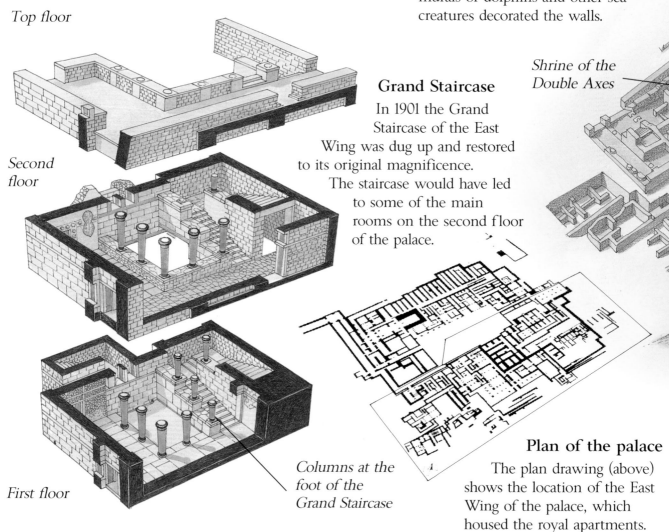

Top floor

Second floor

First floor

Grand Staircase

In 1901 the Grand Staircase of the East Wing was dug up and restored to its original magnificence. The staircase would have led to some of the main rooms on the second floor of the palace.

Shrine of the Double Axes

Columns at the foot of the Grand Staircase

Plan of the palace

The plan drawing (above) shows the location of the East Wing of the palace, which housed the royal apartments.

Priest or acrobat?

This mural (right) from Knossos shows the so-called "priest-king." His loincloth, flowing hair and plumed lily crown are more typical of an acrobat than a king.

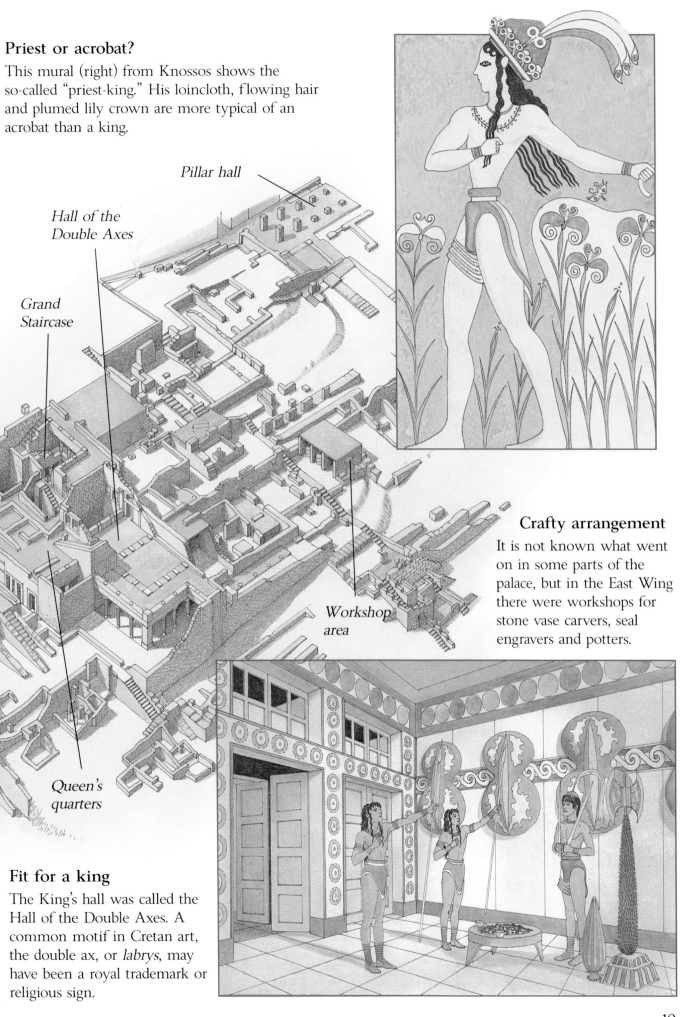

Pillar hall

Hall of the Double Axes

Grand Staircase

Workshop area

Queen's quarters

Crafty arrangement

It is not known what went on in some parts of the palace, but in the East Wing there were workshops for stone vase carvers, seal engravers and potters.

Fit for a king

The King's hall was called the Hall of the Double Axes. A common motif in Cretan art, the double ax, or *labrys*, may have been a royal trademark or religious sign.

19

A working palace

In about 2000BC there was a sudden increase in agricultural production in Crete and it became necessary for the Minoans to measure and record what they produced, as well as to store it in a safe place. They traded goods wherever possible to avoid waste.

The Palace of Knossos provided a central location for storing and administering the produce, which could be made available to the population if there was a bad harvest. A group of dignitaries, scribes, heads of offices and inspectors regulated all production, consignment, storage, distribution and trade.

The palace archives record goods already consigned as well as goods not yet shipped, together with the salaries of the workforce. They list raw materials such as metals and timber, the number of slaves according to age and sex and even sacrifices to the gods.

Jars for olive oil

This procession of jar bearers is from a painted mural in the West Wing. There were at least 400 jars in the palace's storerooms, each one containing olive oil. This meant that huge amounts of oil were stored in the palace at any one time. Olive oil was a valuable commodity in ancient Crete and was used for many purposes, including cooking.

View of storeroom

Palace storage

The storerooms contained stone-lined boxes and large storage jars for olive oil. At one time some of the boxes had been lined with lead for storing clothes and valuables. Large storage jars called pithoi were often decorated with a motif, such as the double ax.

Storage jar with double-ax decorative motif

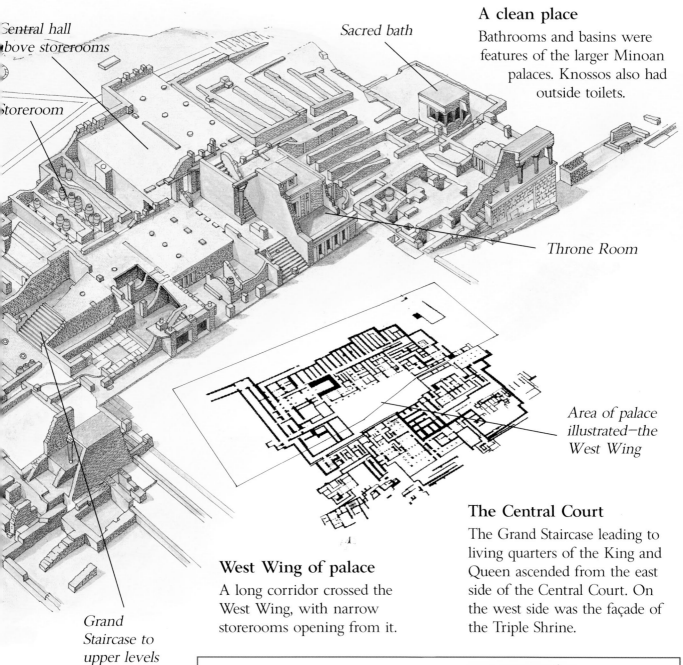

Central hall above storerooms

Storeroom

Sacred bath

A clean place

Bathrooms and basins were features of the larger Minoan palaces. Knossos also had outside toilets.

Throne Room

Area of palace illustrated–the West Wing

Grand Staircase to upper levels

West Wing of palace

A long corridor crossed the West Wing, with narrow storerooms opening from it.

The Central Court

The Grand Staircase leading to living quarters of the King and Queen ascended from the east side of the Central Court. On the west side was the façade of the Triple Shrine.

Triple Shrine façade

The façade of the West Wing overlooked the Central Court of the palace. Behind the façade was the Triple Shrine and a room with boxes sunk into the floor, where the Minoans kept their idols and other sacred objects used in religious ceremonies. This area of the palace was rebuilt during the excavations.

The sea kingdom

The Minoan civilization relied on sea power for its defense and sea trading for its prosperity. No large fortifications were ever built by the Minoans, but ancient Crete had many important ports scattered around the island.

The power of the last rulers of Crete extended to other islands in the Aegean. Melos, Thera Kea and most of all Thera show strong cultural similarities and it is likely that they came under Minoan rule for at least some time. Important cities such as Gournia grew up on the coast of Crete, and by 1550BC there were good roads linking them.

Knossos was at the center of this empire, with the palace acting not only as a king's residence but also a seat of administration for the island.

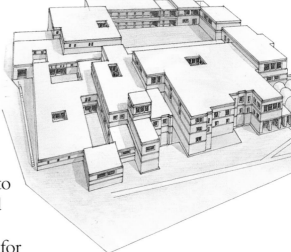

The palace of Mallia
The three main palaces of the Minoan kingdom were Knossos, Phaistos and a small but very rich one at Mallia.

State vessel
This magnificent vessel is a state boat from the nearby island of Thera.

Palaces and ports
The Palace of Knossos was at the center of the great sea power of the Minoans. The town was protected from sea attack by a fleet of warships. There were smaller, less important palaces all over the island of Crete, such as those at Phaistos and Mallia, as well as several important ports for sea trade.

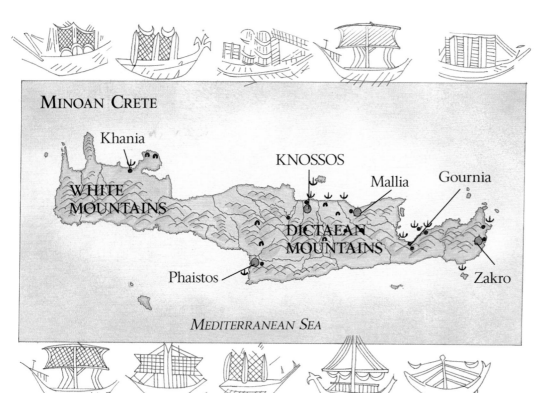

MINOAN CRETE

Khania

KNOSSOS

Mallia

Gournia

WHITE MOUNTAINS

DICTAEAN MOUNTAINS

Phaistos

Zakro

MEDITERRANEAN SEA

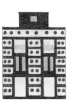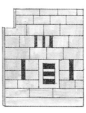

All shapes and sizes

A typical Minoan house was built to fit the space available in the town. These Minoan plaques show six different house styles.

Roads and streets

A good road system connected the palaces of Crete with outlying towns, villages and individual farms. Streets in the towns were narrow and had a raised sidewalk for pedestrians, who would dart sideways to avoid carts, wagons or the occasional royal litter.

Working town

Gournia was a busy artisans' town, where the people produced fine examples of pottery and other craftware for the great palaces of Knossos and Phaistos.

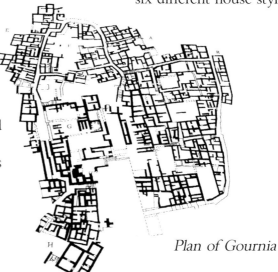

Plan of Gournia

STREET SCENE IN GOURNIA

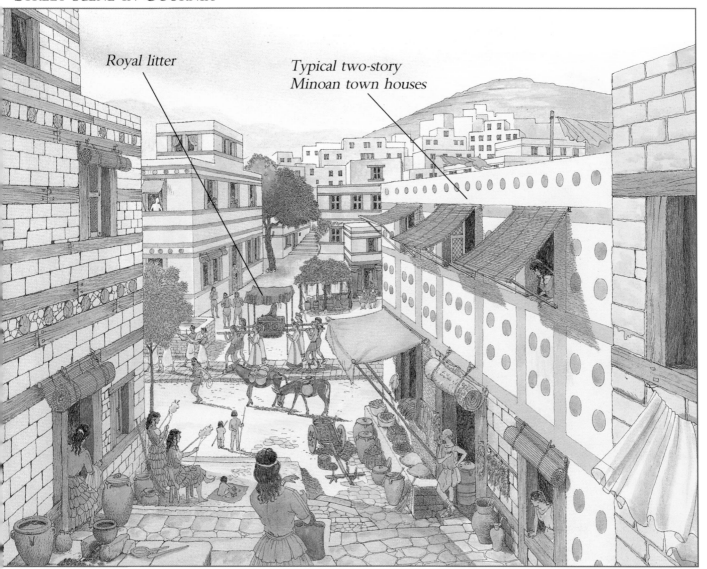

Royal litter

Typical two-story Minoan town houses

Trade and writing

In Minoan times the production and distribution of goods were controlled by the priests and the royal family, who were the only traders.

The palace administration traded with the rulers of other countries. Raids on passing ships and on far-off lands provided most of the wealth in the royal treasury—perhaps more than the exchange of products.

Accounts listing goods and commodities were written on tablets in hieroglyphics and other, later scripts. The tablets show how meticulously the economy was controlled by the palace accountants.

A jar bearer

Copper ingots

In the late Bronze Age, large copper ingots were used instead of money for exchanging goods. They were made in the shape of animal hides, with inward-curving sides for carrying on the shoulder. The trident sign on these ingots from Knossos represented Poseidon, the Greek god of the sea.

Pictorial writing   *"Linear A"*   *"Linear B"*

Signs and symbols

Early Minoans (c 2500BC) developed a form of pictorial writing on clay tablets. The tablets were thought to be accounts listing goods. Some signs were numerals; others represented objects. Later, the "Linear A" script was developed. "Linear B" script may have come with invaders from Greece in 1450BC.

A scribe in the archive

Scribes kept written records using pens. Ink came from squids or cuttlefish.

"Linear A" script

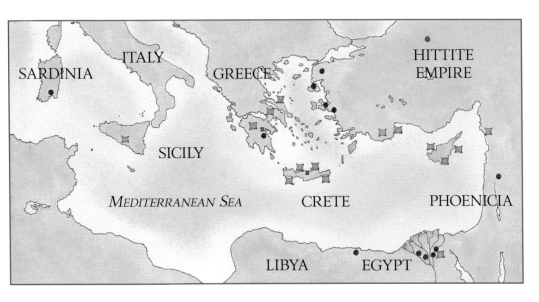

Cretan trade

About 1450BC the Minoans were trading with other countries. On the map (left), the red ingots represent where archaeologists have found Minoan copper ingots, and the black dots represent finds of other goods, such as pottery and olive oil.

Fair exchange

The Minoans exchanged swords for ostrich eggs from Libya. They exported timber, woven wool and linen, daggers, stone lamps and vases, pottery and metal vessels. Copper was imported from Anatolia (Turkey) and Cyprus; gold from Egypt and Kush (Ethiopia).

Oil for artefacts

Minoan envoys to Egypt took vessels containing scented oils. In return they were given stone vases and other gifts to take back.

1. Metal vessels
2. Stone oil lamp
3. Sword and daggers

4./5. Jar and scarab seal from Egypt
6. Minoan merchant ships (from seal impressions at Knossos)
7. Drinking cup
8. Stone vases
9. Vase

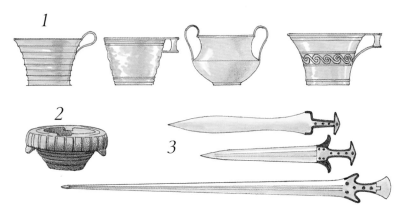

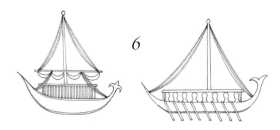

The farming year

Crete has three climatic seasons: the rainy season, from November to February; the flowering season, from March to June; and the dry season, from July to October.

At the start of the rainy season, the flocks came down from the mountains, olives were picked from the trees to make oil and grapes to make wine. Crops were sown from November to April and harvested from May to August.

Milk and meat came from cattle, sheep and goats, and hunting supplied more meat from wild animals such as deer and boar. The Minoans had terraced fields and built dams to preserve rainwater, but they practiced agriculture without irrigation, and relied on rain to water their crops.

For a society based on agriculture, a reliable calendar was essential and the Minoan calendar was well thought out.

Zyzyphus sativa   *Arbutus*   *Ha*

Farmer's script

The signs of the "Linear B" script, used by the Minoans, recorded anything to do with agriculture, such as food crops and animals.

Wheat   Barley   Olive oil   Figs   Spices

Ox   Cow   Sheep   Goat   Pig   Donkey   Horse   Deer

Festival of fruits

The picture above shows a Minoan harvest festival procession, as well as the types of wild fruits that provided much of the island's food.

Clay animals

Donkeys and oxen worked the land and transported the produce. Working oxen were often given pet names such as "Brownie," "Blondie" or "Reddie."

Pots for cooking

Farmers ate a simple diet of soups and stews, cooked over an open fire. Meat was only eaten after an animal had been sacrificed to the gods.

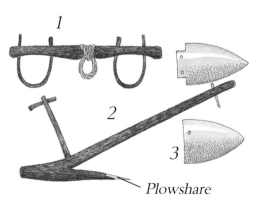

Caldron and ladle

Stove

Cup

Funr

Egg tray   *Grill*

Tools for plowing

To prepare the ground for sowing, the Minoans used wooden plows and yokes.

1. Yoke
2. Plow
3. Plowshares

Plowshare

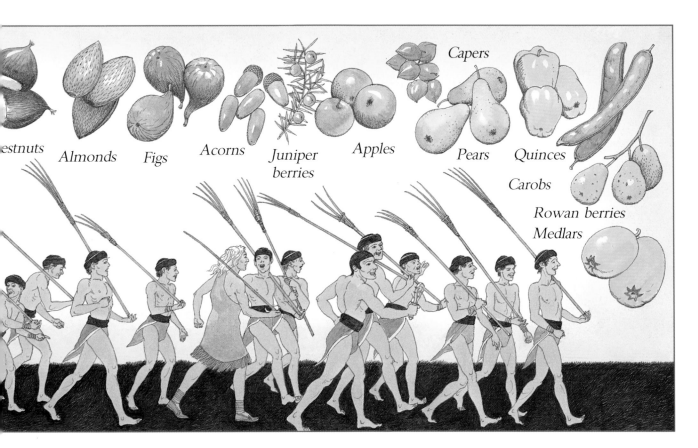

estnuts Almonds Figs Acorns Juniper berries Apples Capers Pears Quinces Carobs Rowan berries Medlars

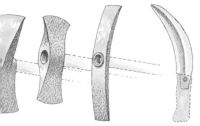

dz-ax Ax Hoe Pruning knife

Bronze implements

The most common tools of Bronze Age Crete were an all-purpose adz-ax, an ax blade for cutting trees and clearing undergrowth, a hoe for weeding and a pruning knife for fruit trees.

Harvesting

June was harvest time in ancient Crete. The farm workers used curved wooden sickles with flint or obsidian blades to cut the grain and long wooden forks to winnow it after threshing.

Winnowing fork

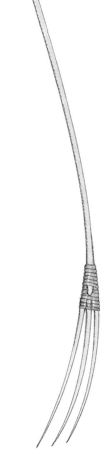

Society and costume

 King Minos was not only a priest-king; he was more like a god-king who played a religious role in Minoan life. He also led the army, owned vast estates and administered justice.

Minoan society consisted of priests, warriors, craftsmen, shepherds and farmers. There were also peasants, who could be bought and sold by the landowners, and serfs (for example soldiers and farm workers) who belonged to the state. Most people had the right to own a house and livestock and could legally marry and divorce.

Women played an important part in Minoan life, particularly in religious ceremonies. The everyday clothes and elaborate hairstyles of the Minoans appear extraordinarily modern to our eyes.

Minoan dancer

Villa at Sklavokampos

Wealthy people lived in country mansions like this one at Sklavokampos. Villas such as this may have had all the amenities and decoration of great town houses.

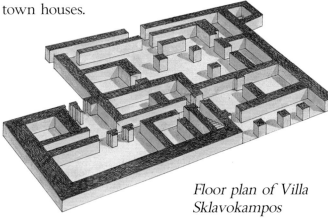

Floor plan of Villa Sklavokampos

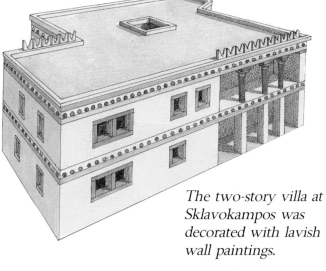

The two-story villa at Sklavokampos was decorated with lavish wall paintings.

Women in blue

The Minoans depicted themselves as slender, dark-haired and very athletic people, with narrow waists and broad shoulders. Women, like men, wore their hair long and flowing (right), with locks hanging down on either side of their face in front of their ears. Among the ruling classes the bolero, or short jacket, was very fashionable.

Clothes worn by men and women in early Minoan Crete, 2500BC

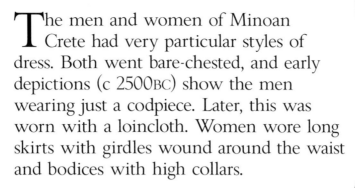

The men and women of Minoan Crete had very particular styles of dress. Both went bare-chested, and early depictions (c 2500BC) show the men wearing just a codpiece. Later, this was worn with a loincloth. Women wore long skirts with girdles wound around the waist and bodices with high collars.

Codpiece

Clay figurines of a woman and man from 2000BC

Headgear

Men wore wide flat caps, or ones with rolled brims, to protect them from the sun and rain.

Height of fashion

The Snake Goddess from Knossos (right) wears a short-sleeved bodice and a long skirt with an apron back and front.

Courtly dress

The style of men's dress at court was a more elaborate loincloth, usually held in place by a girdle or belt. It could be worn as a kilt or folded like a pair of shorts.

1

3

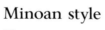

2

Minoan style

The costumes of men and women in Bronze Age Crete are depicted in bronze and clay figurines and wall paintings of the time.
1. Bronze statues wearing typical costumes.
2. Clay model of boot and a Greek sandal.
3. Detail of man's costume in 1.
4. Woman from Thera in a typical skirt.

4

Arts and crafts

The great palaces of Crete, of which Knossos was the finest, were decorated with magnificent gypsum carvings, painted stucco reliefs and delicate polished tiles that showed a high level of craftsmanship in every field.

Minoan stone vases, some with carved handles and metal parts, were extremely elegant, and Minoan pottery is among the most beautiful ever produced in the ancient world.

The Minoans were great observers of nature and decorated their vases with drawings of fish, birds, animals and flowers. Minoan gold and silver jewelry, too, demonstrated a high level of skill.

Painting and carving

Pictures painted on walls and pottery usually showed people or animals in profile, like this woman called *La Parisienne* in the Palace of Knossos. Decorative carving in gypsum was also popular.

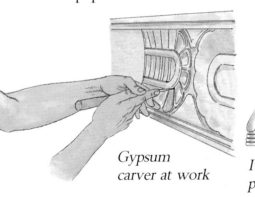

Gypsum carver at work

Ivory game piece

Games of art

A game board (above) from the Palace of Knossos was nearly three feet (one meter) long. It was made of ivory, covered with gold and inlaid with stones and glass paste.

Tilers cut stone tiles using an adz with a handle.

1 *2* *3*

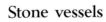

Stone vessels

Cretan stone vases ranged in size from miniatures to large storage vessels.
1. Rock crystal vase
2. Vertically fluted vase
3. Spouted jar in porphyry

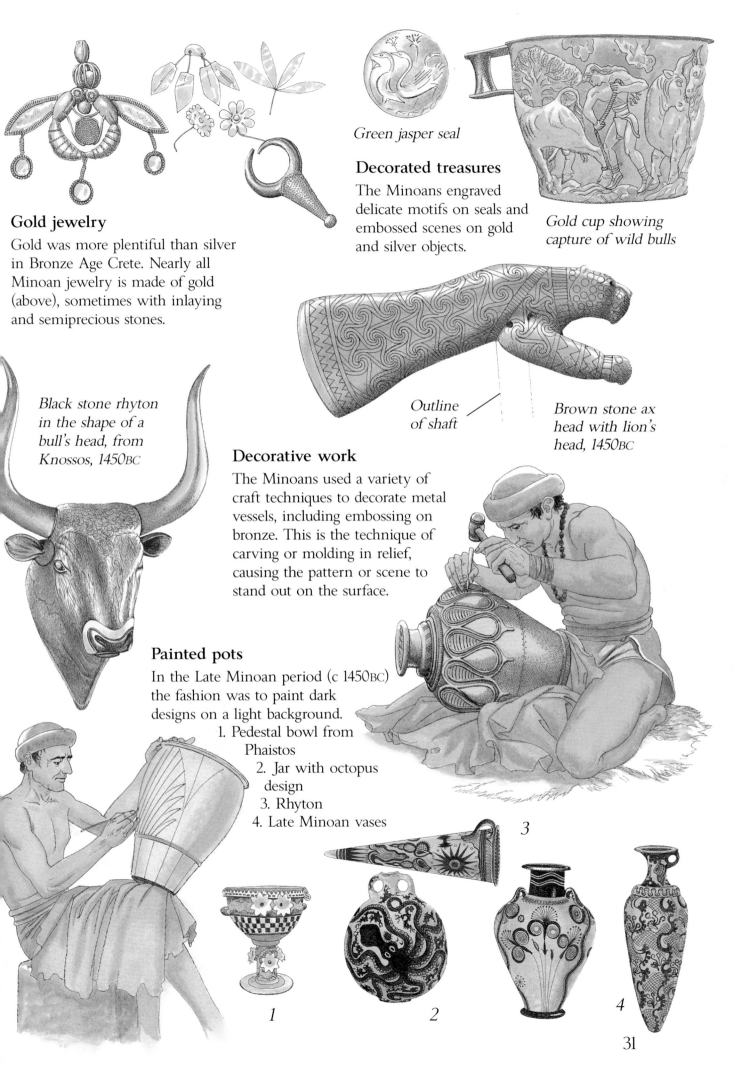

Gold jewelry

Gold was more plentiful than silver in Bronze Age Crete. Nearly all Minoan jewelry is made of gold (above), sometimes with inlaying and semiprecious stones.

Green jasper seal

Decorated treasures

The Minoans engraved delicate motifs on seals and embossed scenes on gold and silver objects.

Gold cup showing capture of wild bulls

Black stone rhyton in the shape of a bull's head, from Knossos, 1450BC

Outline of shaft

Brown stone ax head with lion's head, 1450BC

Decorative work

The Minoans used a variety of craft techniques to decorate metal vessels, including embossing on bronze. This is the technique of carving or molding in relief, causing the pattern or scene to stand out on the surface.

Painted pots

In the Late Minoan period (c 1450BC) the fashion was to paint dark designs on a light background.

1. Pedestal bowl from Phaistos
2. Jar with octopus design
3. Rhyton
4. Late Minoan vases

1

2

3

4

Religion

Unlike some other civilizations, the Minoans did not build huge temples. They worshiped their gods in small sanctuaries and shrines where the only essential feature was a column supporting the ceiling.

Each house had its own sanctuary or shrine, and the pillar was the center of worship. It was also the main support of the house, protecting it from earthquakes.

Many Minoan communities had their own hilltop sanctuary, where people would leave offerings to the gods. Caves and grottoes in the mountains of Crete were often sanctuaries or cult sites; and special rooms in palaces, as well as in ordinary houses, were used as cult places. They contained incense burners and small domed altars.

Gift for the gods

In a scene depicting the sacrifice of a bull, a priestess at the altar offers a drink to the gods. Behind her, a pipe player stands beside the trussed bull.

Cult objects included double axes, bulls' horns and clay figurines of goddesses and worshipers.

Snake Goddess

The Minoans worshiped a chief female deity, who was a snake handler. The bare-breasted goddess and priestesses of her cult held up snakes, which coiled around their bodies and arms.

Double ax

The double ax, which appears throughout Minoan culture, may have been a religious symbol or royal trademark. This gold one is from the palace at Zakro.

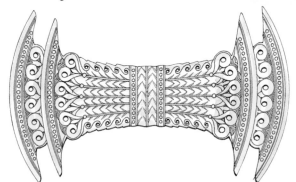

The Minoan bull

The bull was one of the chief objects of worship in ancient Crete, and bull's horns were a common religious symbol. It was also the most frequent victim of animal sacrifice. This wall painting (right) from Knossos shows three youths somersaulting over a bull in the bull-leaping ritual.

Dangerous acrobatics

A kind of bullfighting was practiced as a religious ritual. This involved male and female acrobats leaping over an angry, running bull.

Perfect landing

Bull-leaping required great skill and courage on the part of the acrobats. Facing the moving bull, the acrobat would grab its horns, leap into the air, and somersault over the top of them onto the bull's back. From this standing position, he or she somersaulted over the bull's tail and landed, feet together, behind the bull.

Family tomb

People's remains were placed inside terracotta lidded chests and buried in family tombs underground.

Burial chest with lid

At the tomb

Worshipers present their offerings at a tomb (left), in front of which stands the dead man.

Ceremonial pose

At religious ceremonies worshipers stood at attention with their right hands held across their foreheads. They watched the priest, who brandished a bronze ax as he prepared to perform the sacrifice. The victim was usually a bull that had been part of the bull-leaping ceremony.

Underground tomb

War and weapons

The palaces, villas and towns on Crete had no fortifications. Either Minoan society did not expect to be invaded or it was not a warlike one. Perhaps the distance between the island and potential enemies was too great, and no doubt the Minoan navy helped to prevent invaders from setting foot on the island.

However, in about 1450BC all the great palaces of Crete, except for Knossos, were destroyed. Knossos continued to exist until about 1370BC, when it was destroyed by fire. Historians do not know whether invaders from Greece took over Knossos and destroyed the other centers or the rulers of Knossos conquered the rest of the island.

Seal impression of chariot drawn by goats, 1500BC

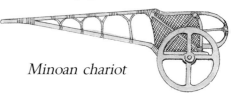

Minoan chariot

The Chieftain cup

This stone cup from the town of Hagia Triada shows a young warrior holding a staff, facing a soldier with two swords. The picture probably tells the story of the initiation of a new recruit to the Minoan army.

Chariots, goats and horses

Wheeled vehicles were in use in Crete from at least 2000BC. Judging by the above seal impression from Knossos, they were sometimes drawn by goats instead of horses. In fact there is no evidence that horses existed in Crete until the fifth century BC. Later, chariots were drawn by horses.

The Minoan soldier

Minoan kings had a small body of foot soldiers at their disposal. Body armor was rarely worn, but the soldiers had helmets made of thick leather, sometimes with a bronze skullcap or strengthened with rows of boars' tusks.

Helmet covered with boars' tusks, from Knossos

Bronze helmet from Knossos

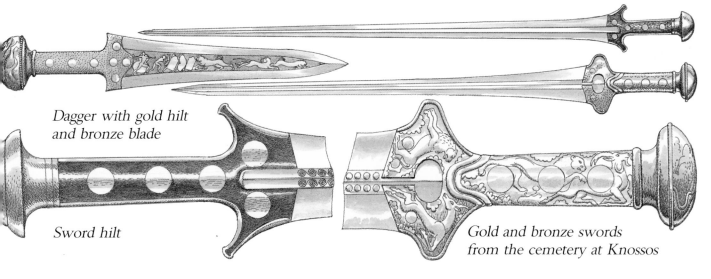

Dagger with gold hilt and bronze blade

Sword hilt

Gold and bronze swords from the cemetery at Knossos

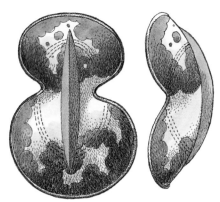

Minoan shields appear to have been made from ox-hides, which were stretched over a wooden frame.

War was a business to be carried out each spring and fall. As a maritime power, Crete defended itself from pirates and competitors and pillaged distant shores, taking prisoners as slaves. The booty was shared among the palace inhabitants, who gave portions to the soldiers, priests and priestesses, and to all their subjects. Weapons included bronze daggers, swords, axes and spearheads.

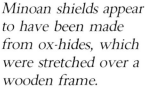

A Minoan warship on an early vase

A tough lot

The Minoan warrior was tested for courage and strength. He was taught to fight and how to tame wild bulls. These boxing figures are taken from a relief on a Minoan vase.

The relief pictures on this stone rhyton from Hagia Triada show youths involved in martial arts.

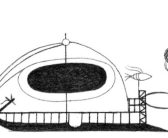

Minoan legacy

The first great civilization that existed on European soil—the Minoans of Crete—was unknown to early 19th-century archaeologists. When Heinrich Schliemann uncovered the cities of Troy and Mycenae, scholars realized that a civilization had existed on Crete long before the Greeks. However, it was not until Evans and his team discovered and reconstructed much of Knossos that the importance of the Minoan civilization was fully recognized.

After its collapse in around 1200BC, it was another 300 years before the Greeks rose to prominence. In many ways their glory was due to the Minoans, who had left them a legacy on which to build.

Walls of symbolism
The walls of Knossos feature enormous pairs of limestone horns, giving an idea of the importance of the bull in Minoan culture.

Strong and sturdy
This view of part of the sacred bath shows the large decorated supporting columns and massive stone construction found throughout Knossos.

Fit for a king
The throne room at Knossos is impressive in its size. Situated against the end wall is the throne of Minos.

Stunning vessel

This elaborate and beautifully crafted rhyton (drinking vessel) is made in the shape of a bull's head. The horns are made of solid gold.

Huge scale

The above view of the reconstructed central area of Knossos gives some idea of the enormous size of the palace.

Colorful art

This restored mural depicting two ancients shows the delicate colors used by the team of restorers.

Going up

The Grand Staircase at Knossos is made from finely hewn blocks of stone and is a remarkable feat of engineering.

Chronology

BC

6000 All the Mediterranean islands, including Crete, are settled by farmers.

3500 Beginning of first urban civilization at Uruk in Mesopotamia.

3250 Writing develops in Mesopotamia.

c 3000 Beginning of the Bronze Age. Earliest hieroglyphic writing in Egypt.

3000 **Early Minoan Period**. The people living on Crete begin to evolve a distinctive culture.

Harvest time in ancient Crete

2650 The first pyramid built in Egypt, at Saqqara.

2200 **Middle Minoan Period**. Birth of the first European civilization, on Minoan Crete. Minoans begin to live in towns.

1950 **First Palace Period**. The palaces of Knossos, Mallia, Zakro and Phaistos are built.

1900 The first writing appears in Crete.

1780 The first Palace at Knossos is destroyed by an earthquake.

1700 **Second Palace Period**. Knossos rebuilt. "Linear A" script appears.

c 1550 A volcanic explosion destroys the island of Thera. Throughout the Aegean Sea, islands are covered with ash and debris, causing catastrophic crop failure. A tsunami—a huge wave caused by an earthquake or volcanic activity—crashes into northern Crete, causing enormous destruction.

State barge from Thera

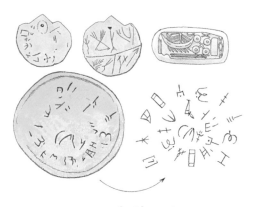

1450 Start of the **Late Minoan Period**. The first cities are built in Greece, and the Mycenaean (early Greek) civilization emerges. Mycenaeans probably invade Crete and destroy palaces, including Knossos.

c 1450 Palaces on Crete are rebuilt. "Linear B" script appears in both Crete and Greece.

1370 Final destruction of Knossos.

Pictorial writing (left) and "Linear A" script

1150 Collapse of civilization in Crete.

700 The Greek poet Homer writes about King Minos in his epics the *Odyssey* and the *Iliad*.

500 Cities on Crete are engaged in rivalry and piracy.

67 Crete conquered by Rome; the island becomes part of the Roman Empire's province of Cyrenacia.

AD

324 Crete becomes part of the Byzantine Empire.

1204 Crete conquered first by the city-states of Genoa and then by Venice.

1669 Crete conquered by the Ottoman (Turkish) Empire.

1821 Cretan war of independence.

1830 Crete is ruled by the Turkish Viceroy of Egypt.

1894 Arthur Evans arrives at Knossos, and determines to excavate the palace.

1898 Crete becomes independent and Prince George of Greece is appointed High Commissioner.

1900 Evans's important series of excavations begins at Knossos.

Evans's book on Cretan pictographs

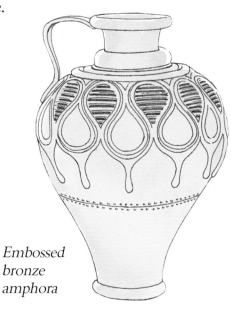

Embossed bronze amphora

Glossary

adz A tool with its metal cutting head at a right angle to the handle.

archaeologist A person who studies the past and excavates the ruins and remains of ancient civilizations in order to learn more about them.

bolero A short jacket, ending above the waist.

capital The top of a column, often decorated.

codpiece A piece of clothing designed to cover the male genitals.

colonnade A row of columns, usually supporting a ceiling, roof or beam of some kind.

A row of painted pine columns from Knossos

Minoan female costume featured a short jacket open down the front to the waist

filigree A pattern or object made by interlacing fine wires.

foundry A place where ores are melted and made into metal.

gypsum A white stone. Crushed, it is used to make plaster.

hieroglyphic A form of writing in which words are represented by symbols, which may look like the object or animal being described.

ingot A piece of pure solid metal, created by pouring molten metal into a mold.

labyrinth An elaborate maze. The labyrinth built by King Minos on Crete contained the Minotaur monster.

Linear A The earliest form of Cretan writing, dating from 1700BC.

Linear B A later form of Cretan and Greek writing, dating from c 1450BC.

litter A stretcherlike object. Carried by bearers, litters were used to transport important people in ancient times.

megaron A large colonnaded reception hall in an ancient Mediterranean palace.

Minoan Referring to the ancient civilization on the island of Crete.

Minos An ancient Cretan king. Greek myth refers to King Minos as if he was one person, but scholars now believe "Minos" was simply a title, such as "Pharaoh" in ancient Egypt.

mural A wall painting.

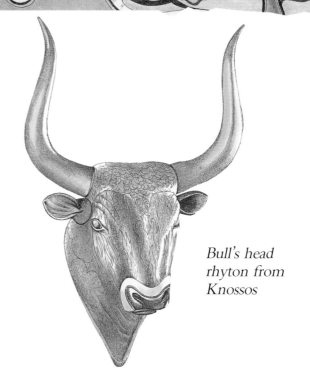

Bull's head rhyton from Knossos

Procession with jars of olive oil

pictographs A form of writing that uses small pictures instead of letters.

pithoi Large Cretan or Greek storage jars.

pottery Drinking vessels, bowls or storage jars made of clay, often decorated, then fired in a kiln to harden them for use.

rhyton An elaborate ancient drinking vessel, often in the shape of an animal's head.

sanctuary A special place where ancient people worshiped their gods.

serf A person who is obligated to provide work, such as agricultural labor, without pay.

stucco Plaster rendering on a wall or other surface, often textured and painted.

winnow To separate kernels of grain from the husks surrounding them.

Elaborate gold drinking cup from Crete

Who's who in the Knossos story

Ariadne Daughter of King Minos, she helped Theseus to slay the Minotaur by providing him with a sword with which to kill the beast, and a ball of thread to help him find his way out of the labyrinth. Theseus married Ariadne and sailed away with her, but later deserted her on the island of Naxos.

Arthur Evans (1851-1941) The British archaeologist who excavated the Palace of Knossos from 1900 on. Son of a wealthy paper manufacturer and antiquarian, Evans wrote works on the Balkan area and coin-collecting before his important work on Crete.

D(avid) G(eorge) Hogarth (1862-1929) English archaeologist who advised Evans in his work at Knossos. He was keeper of the Ashmolean Museum at Oxford from 1909 to 1927, and excavated sites in Syria, Asia Minor and Egypt.

Minos King of the island of Crete. Most scholars today believe that "Minos" did not refer to one person, and that there were actually several King Minoses.

Arthur Evans searches for carved seals in Crete during the 1890s

Minotaur The hideous monster, half-human, half-bull, born to Minos's wife as a result of the displeasure of Poseidon, the sea god, when Minos kept back a bull destined for sacrifice to the god. Kept in a labyrinth (maze), the Minotaur demanded a tribute of seven boys and seven girls every nine years.

Poseidon In ancient Greek myth, the powerful god of the sea. He was the son of Cronus and Rhea and the brother of Zeus.

Theseus According to legend Theseus was the son of King Aegeus of Athens and the Princess Aethra. Theseus was renowned for his heroism, and could not bear the fact that seven boys and girls had to be sacrificed every nine years to the Minotaur. Volunteering to sail to Crete and become one of the monster's victims, Theseus found his way through the labyrinth with the help of Ariadne and slew the beast.

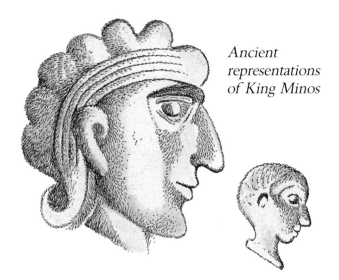

Ancient representations of King Minos

Index

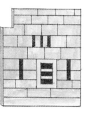